INSPIRING ARTISTS

VINCENT VAN GOGH

Published in 2016 by The Rosen Publishing Group, Inc.
29 East 21st Street, New York, NY 10010

First Edition

Library of Congress Cataloging-in-Publication Data

Ruth Thomson.
Vincent Van Gogh / Ruth Thomson. -- First Edition.
pages cm. -- (Inspiring artists)
Includes index.
ISBN 978-1-5081-7056-3 (library bound)
1. Gogh, Vincent van, 1853-1890--Juvenile literature. 2. Painters--Netherlands--Biography--Juvenile literature. I. Title.
ND653.G7T48 2016
759.9492092--dc23
2015034959

Manufactured in the United States of America

INSPIRING ARTISTS
VINCENT VAN GOGH

Ruth Thomson

ROSEN
PUBLISHING®
New York

Every attempt has been made to clear copyright. Should there be any inadvertent omission please apply to the publisher for rectification.

CONTENTS

Beginnings

Today, Vincent van Gogh is considered one of the founders of modern art. His expressive pictures of nature, ordinary people and everyday things, with paint as thick as toothpaste, vibrant colors and often distorted forms, have inspired many successive artists.

Artistic temperament

Van Gogh was sensitive, passionate and eccentric. Always short of money, often despairing and lonely, he also had recurring attacks of depression and hallucinations (seeing things that are not there). Painting was his way of expressing who he was and how he felt. He usually painted very quickly, creating more than 2,000 artworks in a career lasting less than 10 years. In van Gogh's lifetime, his work was hardly known to the public and scarcely sold. Collectors dismissed his works as those of a madman.

Youth

It was not obvious that van Gogh would become an artist. Born in 1853, he grew up in a clergyman's family in the flat countryside of the southern Netherlands, showing no special talent for drawing. His early passions were nature and religion.

At the age of 16, van Gogh joined Goupil and Co., his uncle's art dealing company in the Hague. After four years, he moved to their branch in London, then to Paris. During his seven years buying and selling art, van Gogh saw the latest trends in art and visited museums to see works by great artists.

Self-portrait, 1887

As he became increasingly religious, van Gogh was dismissed from his job. Wanting to do good, he worked first as a teacher, then as a preacher among the poor. At the age of 27, van Gogh decided to become an artist. He hoped his work might bring joy and comfort to people.

Heads of the People: The Coastguardsman, Hubert von Herkomer, 1879

6

Wheat Fields, Jacob van Ruisdael, c.1670

In museums in the Netherlands, Paris and London, van Gogh studied works by great Dutch painters – sweeping landscapes by Jacob van Ruisdael (1628–1682) and moving portraits by Rembrandt (1606–1669). He also admired works by Eugène Delacroix (1798–1863) and Jean-François Millet (1814–1875).

Early artistic influences

While in London, van Gogh discovered weekly magazines with engravings of events and features. He also collected illustrations showing the life of the poor. Hubert von Herkomer (1849–1914) drew and painted heads of workers, including a coastguard (opposite, bottom) and a miner. This inspired van Gogh's own portraits of peasant heads (see p.12).

Letters

Van Gogh frequently wrote letters to his brother Theo, his sister and his artist friends. These vividly describe his struggles to draw and paint, ideas for paintings and choice of colors, the art he admired and his views on news events. Many of his letters requested or thanked Theo for money, as Theo supported him financially throughout his artistic life.

Letter dated August 4, 1884 from van Gogh to his brother Theo, saying that his figure drawing was improving daily.

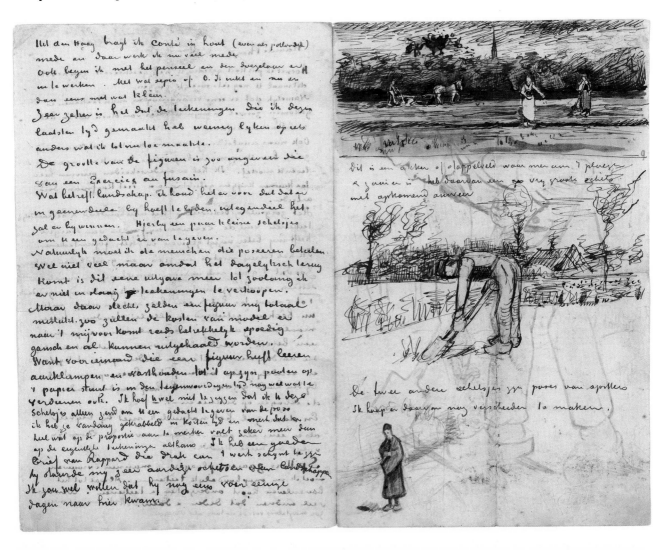

Becoming an artist

For several years, from 1880, van Gogh determinedly set to work every day, learning basic drawing skills in pencil, pen and ink, and black chalk. At this time, he was living at his parents' home in Etten, where, in good weather, he roamed the countryside, drawing landscapes, farm buildings and tools.

Honing his skills

Van Gogh's brother Theo, now working at Goupil's in Paris, sent him prints to copy and books of figure-drawing exercises, which van Gogh repeatedly practiced, especially when the weather was too rainy for sketching outdoors.

He drew people at work on the land, using locals as models, as in *Digger* (right). He also practiced mastering perspective, using a wooden perspective frame with criss-crossed wires that make a grid. This device helped him achieve the impression of distance in his landscapes, as in his exercise *Road in Etten* (below).

Road in Etten, 1881

Digger, 1885

Oil painting

As van Gogh's skills improved, he moved to the Hague, hoping to meet other artists. His cousin Anton Mauve (1838–1888), a successful painter of Dutch country scenes, gave him lessons in painting in watercolors and oils.

8

Milking Time, Anton Mauve, 1875.

Remote inspiration

In 1883, fleeing a failed love affair, van Gogh spent several months in Drenthe, remote, empty, and windswept moorlands in the north of the Netherlands. Here, poor peat cutters lived in mean sod cottages and toiled in all weather. In his painting *Two Peasant Women in the Peat Field* (below), van Gogh used broad bands of gloomy color with very few details, summing up the bleakness of this landscape as well as his own despair and loneliness.

Art *How does van Gogh's depiction of farm workers differ from Mauve's? Which gives you more of a feeling of peasant life?*

Women on the Peat Moor, 1883

A peasant painter

Above all, van Gogh wanted to be a painter of peasant life, depicting the harsh, tiring, repetitive life of farm workers, miners and weavers in a realistic way. He admired the peasants' harmony with nature, toiling in all weather and seasons, and believed that hard, honest work was the greatest expression of spirituality.

The Sower (after Millet), 1881

Jean-François Millet

Van Gogh was inspired by the French artist, Jean-François Millet, who painted a series of large pictures of farm laborers in the mid-19th century. At that time, it was far more usual to paint pictures of the rich and notable than the poor and humble. Millet was the first artist to show peasants prominently as the subjects of pictures, rather than as tiny figures in the background of a landscape.

The Sower, Jean-François Millet, 1850

Copies

Millet painted pictures of peasants digging, planting potatoes, hoeing, harvesting and gleaning (gathering leftover grain) at different times of year. Van Gogh particularly admired Millet's painting *The Sower* (below left), which showed a muscular man striding across a field, scattering seeds from a cloth sack. The figure takes up almost the entire picture. Van Gogh made dozens of copies of Millet's work (above) before he felt confident enough to draw workers in action from life (below). Like Millet, van Gogh drew his sower large and placed him centrally in the picture. He also copied the pose of Millet's sower, with his right arm back and his right foot forward, but here the sower's movement looks far stiffer.

The Sower, 1882

Weaver Standing at a Loom, 1884

Art

How does van Gogh's drawing of a sower differ from the copy he made of Millet's sower?

Ploughman with Woman Planting Potatoes, 1884.

Rural life

During this time, van Gogh painted many pictures of poor home weavers, working on hand looms. These showed a dying rural craft, which was being taken over by power looms in factories. He also worked outside, painting scenes of the simple country tasks he so admired – digging, planting, weeding, lifting potatoes and sugar beets, and reaping wheat.

The Potato Eaters

In van Gogh's time, peasants worked by hand, from dawn to dusk, come rain or shine. They lived in dark, cramped homes and ate the food they grew. In *The Potato Eaters* van Gogh decided to create a forceful painting showing how tough peasant life was. The painting shows three generations of a tired peasant family sitting at a table, sharing a simple evening meal of boiled potatoes with black coffee by the light of an oil lamp.

"I have really wanted to make it so that people get the idea that these folk, who are eating their potatoes by lamplight, have tilled the earth themselves with these hands they are putting in the dish, so it speaks of manual labor and they have honestly earned their food."
–van Gogh

Study of Three Hands, Two Holding Forks, 1885

Studies

Before van Gogh started work on the painting, he spent the winter months painting studies of heads (below left) and visiting nearby cottages to draw their interiors. He also drew numerous studies of hands (above).

 **Art**

Van Gogh was inspired by this picture of a peasant family having a meal. How does its view differ from that of The Potato Eaters?

Below left: *Head of a Woman*, 1885

Below: *Peasant Family at Table*, Jozef Israels, 1882

The Finished Painting

Choosing a palette of earthy, muddy browns, reds, grays and black to paint *The Potato Eaters*, van Gogh conveyed the gloom and poverty of the cramped cottage, with its rough wooden table and chairs. He deliberately made the family look worn and ugly, with swarthy, weathered skin, exaggerated features, swollen, knobbly hands and dark, heavy clothes. This was his way of emphasizing the effort it took them to provide the family's food.

The Potato Eaters, 1885

Van Gogh felt this was the best picture he had ever painted. He sent it to Theo in Paris, hoping to sell it. But dealers criticized the painting for showing such ugly people. They did not understand what van Gogh was trying to achieve. The picture seemed dark and old-fashioned, compared with the more colorful art then fashionable in Paris (see p. 14–15).

Art in Paris

As an art dealer in Paris, van Gogh's brother Theo saw the growing popularity of work by artists such as Claude Monet (1840–1926), Pierre-Auguste Renoir (1841–1919) and Alfred Sisley (1839–1899). These artists, known as Impressionists, had developed a new style of painting.

Impressionism

The Impressionists often painted views of bustling Paris and sunny landscapes, mostly done in the open air. They used light, bright, unmixed colors, applying them with separate, distinct, brushstrokes. They explored how paint could suggest fleeting impressions of light, weather and movement through contrasts in color.

Woman With a Parasol, Claude Monet, 1875

Les Grands Boulevards, Pierre-Auguste Renoir, 1875

14

Meadow, Alfred Sisley, 1875

Van Gogh comes to Paris

Theo had tried to convince van Gogh to paint more cheerful, saleable landscapes, using brighter colors like the Impressionists. However, it was only when van Gogh moved to Paris in 1886, that he could see for himself what Impressionist paintings were like.

Art *How many different sorts of brushstrokes can you see in these Impressionist paintings? Which words best describe them – spotty, dashed, round, stumpy, patchy, shivery, speckled, swirly, long, fat, stumpy, twisty, commas?*

Paints and paintbrushes

Impressionism, as well as van Gogh's way of painting, could not have developed without three 19th-century inventions. Artists could now buy a wide range of bright, chemically-produced colors, mixed and sold by specialist merchants. The paints came in metal tubes, which kept them soft and ready for use, even outdoors. New, flat (instead of round) paintbrushes meant that artists could load their paintbrushes more heavily and paint with wide, flat, visible brushstrokes.

Experiments with color

Van Gogh had been interested in the interaction of colors before he arrived in Paris, but once there, under the influence of the French painters, he became totally obsessed with it. He was influenced by the theories of Michel-Eugène Chevreul, a French chemist, who explained, using a color wheel, why some colors placed side by side look brighter together than on their own.

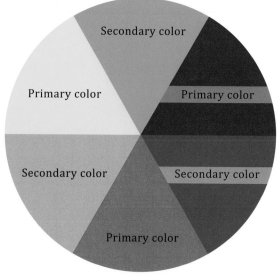

The color wheel

Look at this simple color wheel. Red, blue and yellow are primary colors (which cannot be made from other colors). Opposite each one is a secondary color – orange, green and purple, each made from mixing the two primaries on either side of it. These pairs – yellow/violet, red/green, blue/orange – are called complementary colors. Placed together, these pairs spark against each other, making both colors seem more intense.

Sunday Afternoon on the Island of La Grande Jatte, Georges Seurat, 1883–1886.

Complementary colors

Impressionists used complementary contrasts to suggest the fleeting effects of light and color in nature. The painter Georges Seurat (1859–1891) wanted to create timeless pictures with more solid forms. To do this, he put small spots of contrasting colors side by side, which, from a distance, blend together in the viewer's eye. This slow, precise, scientific technique (known as pointillism) makes everything in his pictures look frozen still, as in *Sunday Afternoon on the Island of La Grande Jatte* (below).

A detail from *Sunday Afternoon on the Island of La Grande Jatte* showing the dots

Clipper at Asnières, Paul Signac, 1887

Trying out techniques

Van Gogh made friends with Paul Signac (1863–1935), another French artist who created his own pointillist paintings. The two artists spent time together painting riverbank scenes on the outskirts of Paris and talking about art.

Signac persuaded van Gogh to abandon his dark palette and to use brighter, clearer, complementary colors instead. Although van Gogh borrowed the Impressionists' dabs and dashes, and mimicked the Pointillists' dots, in the end, he developed a style that was uniquely his own.

Art *What complementary colors can you spot in* Seine Bridge at Asnières *and* Clipper at Asnières?

Seine Bridge at Asnières, 1887

Japanese prints

In the mid-19th century, Japanese art was very fashionable in France. It had a great influence on van Gogh. He bought hundreds of cheap Japanese color prints of everyday life and nature to decorate his room.

Unusual compositions

Van Gogh was impressed by the simple, clear-cut compositions, with large blocks of flat, solid vibrant colors without any shadows. The designs often included strong diagonals and dramatic cropping. Everything was outlined in black.

"All my work to some extent is based on Japanese art." –van Gogh

Flowering Plum Orchard (after Hiroshige), 1887

Plum Estate at Kameido, Utagawa Hiroshige, 1857

Making copies

Van Gogh often learned about a style by copying it. He made copies of three Japanese woodblock prints, including one of a plum tree (above). After drawing a grid on paper, he traced the entire print. He transferred this tracing, detail by detail, on to a larger grid drawn on a canvas, and then painted it (left).

Notice how van Gogh painted the branch dark brownish red, making it stand out. He darkened the red area of the sky and the green ground to exaggerate the three bands of color behind the branch. Unlike the smooth surface of Hiroshige's print, van Gogh's blotchy, oil paint brushstrokes are clearly visible.

Van Gogh's copy of the plum tree was painted on a ready-made canvas, which was not the same proportion as the print. Van Gogh added a colorful border to fill the canvas. He decorated it with random Japanese characters, copied from other prints.

Père Tanguy

Van Gogh painted a portrait of Père Tanguy, his paint merchant, sitting against a backdrop of some of van Gogh's Japanese prints. Van

Portrait of Père Tanguy, 1887

Gogh's colors are much brighter than those he had used before, perhaps influenced by the vividness of the colors in these prints.

Still lifes

As a way of continuing his experiments with color contrasts, van Gogh spent several months painting still lifes of garden flowers. People sent him fresh flowers every week, which he painted rapidly before they faded and died. He also painted still lifes of fruit, vegetables and even his own well-worn boots.

Thick paint

French artist Adolphe Monticelli (1824–1886) painted vividly colored flower pictures like *Bouquet* (below) with thickly encrusted paint (known as impasto) and dark backgrounds.

Van Gogh used the same technique as Monticelli in *Vase with Daisies and Anemones* (below), making each brushstroke visible. He used pure colors straight from the tube. Long diagonal strokes make the table top feel solid, short curved strokes give shape to the vase and dabs or speckles suggest flower petals.

Art *"I have made a series of color studies in painting simply flowers … seeking oppositions of blue with orange, red and green, yellow and violet… I have been trying to convey intense color."* Can you spot the color contrasts that van Gogh describes in Vase with Daisies and Anemones?

Bouquet, Adolphe Monticelli, c.1875

Vase with Daisies and Anemones, 1887

Anna Wied's Flower Garden, Emil Nolde, 1907

Emil Nolde

Emil Nolde (1867–1956) was as fond of flowers as van Gogh. He painted lush flower gardens, individual blooms and bouquets in vases. Following van Gogh's example, Nolde used thick brushstrokes, simplified forms and strong contrasting colors. Nolde was part of *Die Brücke* (The Bridge) group, along with Ernst Ludwig Kirchner (1880–1938) (see p.35) and Erich Heckel (1883–1970) (p.37). Van Gogh's work inspired them to create more personal and emotional art.

Everyday subjects

Van Gogh found interest in painting the most ordinary things – potatoes, cabbages, apples, dried sunflower heads and even shoes and boots. This battered pair, painted in dark tones, is perhaps a reminder of the long walks van Gogh took around his home in the Netherlands.

Shoes, 1887

Self-portraits

During his two years in Paris, van Gogh painted more than 30 self-portraits. He could rarely find or afford models. Painting himself was a way of developing his skills as an artist. His self-portraits were also an expression of his emotions. In times of confidence, he portrayed himself as a smart man about town, wearing a suit, felt or straw hat and silk cravat. In moments of despair and loneliness, he painted himself bare-headed, looking gaunt, worried and sickly.

Self-Portrait with Dark Felt Hat at the Easel, 1886

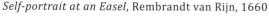
Self-portrait at an Easel, Rembrandt van Rijn, 1660

In Rembrandt's footsteps

Van Gogh revered the 17th-century Dutch artist Rembrandt van Rijn, who painted numerous self-portraits in different poses. Rembrandt's self-portrait as an artist (left) was on show in the Louvre Museum in Paris, which van Gogh often visited. In an early self-portrait (above), van Gogh copied both Rembrandt's dark colors and his half-length pose at an easel.

A modern self-portrait

The last self-portrait that van Gogh painted in Paris shows what he had learned about color, as well as the influence of Impressionism. His palette is encrusted with bright, unmixed colors, and he holds the many flat paintbrushes that he used to create the portrait. His flaming orange beard sings against his blue linen smock, which is flecked with orange to show its coarse texture. The pale gray background helps his head and body stand out.

Self-portrait as a Painter, 1888

In van Gogh's footsteps

The young Spanish artist Pablo Picasso (1881–1973) exhibited his own self-portrait at his first exhibition in Paris in 1901. Picasso holds a palette full of the colors he used to create the portrait just as van Gogh did. The heavy brushstrokes, the unreal colors that make up his face and the dark background setting off his smock are all in homage to van Gogh's way of painting.

Yo Picasso, Pablo Picasso, 1901

Move to the south

In early 1888, van Gogh moved to Arles, a small town in southern France. Once spring came, he eagerly explored his surroundings on foot and painted outdoors in all weather, methodically recording country life season by season, just as he had done in the Netherlands.

Spring themes

In March, van Gogh painted a little bridge over a canal at Langlois (below), intensifying the complementary color contrasts to make the picture sparkle with movement and life. In April, he painted a series of flowering almond, pear and plum orchards. In *The Pink Orchard* (right) he used thick dabs of paint to suggest the tiny blossoms and short brushstrokes for the sprouting grass.

The Pink Orchard, 1888

The Langlois Bridge at Arles with Women Washing, 1888

Farmhouse in Provence (The Farm Gate), 1888

Intense colors

All through the scorching summer, van Gogh painted flower-filled gardens, wheatfields, and haystacks, exaggerating color contrasts to create a sense of shimmering midday heat, with not a shadow in sight. When autumn came, he painted the grape harvest and sowers scattering seed for the following year's crops.

The Fauves

Inspired by van Gogh's vibrant colors and visible brushstrokes, the French artists Maurice de Vlaminck (1876–1958), Henri Matisse (1869–1954) and André Derain (1880–1954) went a step further. They painted scenes with colors that could not be seen in nature at all. Their strong, unnatural colors, bold brushstrokes and the rough, simplified look of their work earned the group the name "Fauves," which means wild beasts.

Art

How has Maurice de Vlaminck used colors to describe light and space in this picture? How has he created a sense of movement?

Potato Pickers, Maurice de Vlaminck, 1905–1907

The modern portrait

One of van Gogh's ambitions was to paint "modern portraits." He was not interested in only capturing his sitters' precise physical likeness. He wanted to create portrait types of ordinary people, which showed something of their life, character and position in society. He hoped that these would be timeless enough to touch viewers long into the future.

"I want to paint men and women with that something of the eternal... which we seek to convey by the actual radiance and vibration of our color."
–van Gogh

Portrait of a peasant

In the portrait *Patience Escalier* (below) van Gogh made a feature of the old man's large, gnarled hands, set against his worn, creased blue smock, to suggest a lifetime spent in hard outdoor work. With his bright red cheeks, the farm laborer looks hot and sweaty from his efforts. The glowing orange background is a reminder of the sweltering summer sun under which peasants brought in the annual harvest.

The Roulin family

Van Gogh's postman neighbour, Joseph Roulin, and his wife, Augustine, were van Gogh's closest friends in Arles. They were both willing models and van Gogh painted many portraits of both them and their children.

La Berceuse

Augustine was the model for van Gogh's image of motherhood which he titled *La Berceuse* (opposite), meaning both the woman who rocks the cradle and the lullaby she sings.

His composition was intended to be particularly comforting. Augustine sits very close to us, the viewers, with her green skirt spreading out of the canvas. The rope she holds is the link between her and the unseen baby being rocked in its cradle. Van Gogh hoped that this might remind viewers of being rocked themselves.

Patience Escalier, 1888

La Berceuse, 1889

Comforting color

Van Gogh outlined Augustine's simple clothes and chair in black and used flat color for her bodice and the floor. The contrasting red and greens were intended to be soothing and the mother's golden face gleams against the riotously flowered wallpaper.

Art *What influences of Japanese art can you spot in this picture?*

Sunflowers

Van Gogh dreamed of setting up an artists' colony, a place where artists could live and work together and share ideas about art. The only artist who agreed to come was Paul Gauguin (1848–1903). Wanting to both impress and welcome Gauguin, van Gogh made a series of joyful sunflower paintings to decorate Gauguin's room.

Sunflowers, 1888

Yellow on yellow

The wall, the table and the earthenware jar, as well as the flowers in *Sunflowers* are all in varying tints of yellow – a novel way of painting. For van Gogh, yellow was a symbol of happiness and hope. The picture seems to radiate brilliant sunlight, reflecting the intensity of the colors that the artist had discovered in the south of France. Van Gogh painted four sunflower pictures in just a week, but only felt satisfied with two of them.

Van Gogh signed this picture, as he did all his others, simply with his first name "Vincent." His name is the decoration on the jar.

Symbolism

Sunflowers were van Gogh's favorite flower, a symbol of the sun, the world's life force. Here, van Gogh shows the sunflowers at different stages of their life cycle – newly coming into flower, in full bloom and gone to seed.

Dabs and dashes

The brushwork echoes the textures and forms of the flowers. The stalks, leaves and petals are painted with long flowing brush strokes in different directions, whereas the seed heads are painted with thick, fat dabs of paint.

A show of sunflowers

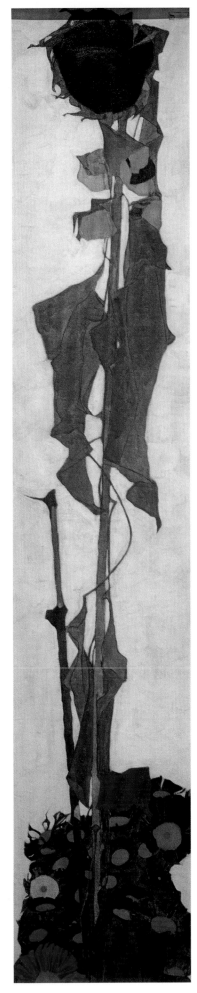

The Sunflower,
Gustav Klimt, 1907

Shown at an exhibition in Vienna in 1906, van Gogh's *Sunflowers* inspired several Austrian artists to paint their own pictures of sunflowers. Gustav Klimt (1862–1918) painted a tall, thriving sunflower growing in an abundant garden border. The sunflower is the majestic centerpiece of his picture, with other, smaller flowers clustered under its leaves. Klimt's style is more decorative than van Gogh's. His picture twinkles with color.

Sunflower II, Egon Schiele, 1910

Egon Schiele's (1890–1918) spindly sunflower is sad and sickly by comparison. The pale leaves are shrivelled and droop limply from the tall stem. The petals have gone, leaving a weighty black head of seeds. Grown far taller than the other flowers, this dying sunflower seems isolated.

Art *Imagine these three pictures of sunflowers are self-portraits of the artists. How would you describe each of their moods?*

Gauguin's visit

Once Gauguin arrived, the two artists went out to work together. They soon began to disagree. Gauguin hated Arles and its cold, windy weather, despised van Gogh's chaotic way of life and criticized his speedy way of painting with thick, visible brushstrokes. Most of all, they argued about the artists they admired and their own inspirations for painting.

Artistic inspiration

Gauguin believed artists should work from their imagination, as he had done in the painting *Vision after the Sermon* (below). This was inspired by religious women whom he saw while living in Brittany, in western France. He imagines these women having a vision of the all-night struggle between the Bible character Jacob and an angel, after having heard a church sermon based on this Bible story. In a letter to van Gogh, Gauguin said of the painting, "For me the landscape and the fight only exist in the imagination of the people praying after the sermon."

Van Gogh found this hard. He was inspired by what he could see – a landscape, an object, a person. Pressured by Gauguin, van Gogh painted *Dance Hall at Arles* (opposite) from memory. With its simplified forms, flat colors and outlines, it seems stiff and joyless compared to many of his other works.

Vision of the Sermon (Jacob Wrestling with the Angel) Paul Gauguin, 1888

Gauguin leaves

Gauguin found van Gogh's strange behavior increasingly unbearable. Van Gogh had frequent outbursts of anger or sulked in moody silence. After repeated arguments and fearful for his own safety, Gauguin decided to leave. Perhaps thinking an act of desperation might persuade Gauguin to stay, van Gogh cut off his earlobe and gave it to someone to pass on to Gauguin. The news of van Gogh's mutilation had the opposite effect. Gauguin fled back to Paris, ruining forever van Gogh's hopes for an artists' colony.

A new palette

In 1892, Gauguin traveled to the Pacific island of Tahiti, seeking to escape modern, industrialised life and find an unspoiled rural environment. The reality was not what he imagined, as the island had long been westernized. Gauguin painted many images of Tahitian women. The heightened colors, especially yellow and blue, show how van Gogh inspired Gauguin to brighten his palette and may also have reflected his exotic new surroundings.

The Dance Hall at Arles, 1888

Nafea Faa Ipoipo (When Will You Marry?), Paul Gauguin, 1892

This is me

When van Gogh returned from several weeks in hospital where he had recovered from his wound, he set about painting almost straightaway. One of the first pictures he painted was a self-portrait.

Me in my studio

In *Self-Portrait with Bandaged Ear* (below) it is a chilly January. Van Gogh looks gaunt and thin in his over-sized thick winter coat and a fur-lined hat, as if he has just come into his studio. He no longer has a beard and his bandaged ear is turned toward us. Behind his head, he has included two things of the greatest importance to him. On the left, a blank canvas on an easel sits waiting for him to paint. Pinned to the wall on the right is one of the Japanese prints that so inspired him.

Self-Portrait with Bandaged Ear, 1889.

Spirals and swirls

Later the same year, van Gogh spent weeks having visions and nightmares, feeling faint, dizzy and fearful. Once he recovered, he painted what was probably his last self-portrait (below). Dressed smartly in a suit, his hair and beard trim, his pose is calm. However, the background quivers with icy blue swirls. We will never know whether these reflect his recent inner turmoil or his newly-found calm.

Art

Every color in van Gogh's head or clothes is matched by a similar color in the background. How many of these can you spot?

Self-portrait, 1889.

Clashes and distortions

The young Austrian artist Oskar Kokoschka
(1886–1980) was inspired by van Gogh's
expressive self-portraits when painting his
own. He, too, believed in trying to show his
inner feelings, rather than creating an exact
likeness of himself. Elongating his face,
enlarging his eyes and hand, and using
clashing reds and sickly greens, he created
a sense of anxiety and agitation.

Close up and far away

Suffering from hallucinations and fits, van Gogh admitted himself to an asylum in Saint Rémy in May, 1889. He stayed there for a year, but managed to produce 142 paintings during that time.

Views from the asylum

At first, van Gogh was allowed out only as far as the asylum's overgrown gardens. Here, he studied flowers and leaves close-up, hoping that concentrating intently on nature would help him get better. In his picture of irises (opposite), each of the leaves has a distinct shape, direction and shade of green, and the grass is painted blade by blade. He also repeatedly painted the view of the walled wheatfield and distant hills that he could see from his room. In *Wheatfield with Reaper* (below) everything, apart from the distant hills, is bathed in a variety of yellows, including the reaper himself.

Art *Van Gogh described the reaper as "a vague figure struggling like the devil in the full heat of the day to reach the end of his toil." How has the artist emphasized the huge amount of work the reaper has to do?*

Wheatfield with a Reaper, 1889.

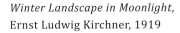
Irises, 1889

Winter moon

The German artist Ernst Ludwig Kirchner (see p.21) followed van Gogh's example, expressing his own response to nature in heightened colors. After the First World War (1914–1918), Kirchner lived high in the Swiss Alps, slowly recovering from the mental breakdown that he had suffered as a soldier. Kirchner also painted the view from his window. Like van Gogh, he simplified the shapes of buildings and trees. He used a limited number of colors – reds, blues and yellows – to create this fantastic moonset. It was, in his words, "amazingly beautiful, but horribly cold."

Winter Landscape in Moonlight, Ernst Ludwig Kirchner, 1919

Expressive lines

Once permitted outside the asylum, van Gogh started painting landscapes around St. Rémy. With groves of knotty olive trees, soaring cypresses and craggy limestone hills, this was very different from the flat land around Arles.

Exaggerated forms

To capture the essence of this new landscape, van Gogh's style changed. He exaggerated the forms of the trees, hills and clouds. Their continuous curves give them rhythmic energy. His brushstrokes now followed one another in waves, curves and swirls. His colors became more muted.

Day and night

Van Gogh planned to display paintings of a daytime scene of olive trees and a night scene side by side. Both pictures feel alive. The old, crooked trees in *The Olive Trees* (below) seem to writhe in the heat against the blue hills.

Only the imaginary village nestling at the foot of the hills is calm in van Gogh's night scene, entitled *The Starry Night* (opposite, bottom). Everything else is moving. The hills surge like waves at sea. The cypress tree quivers and spirals toward the twirling, glittering sky. The whirling circles around the stars and moon seem to make them pulse.

The Olive Trees, 1889.

Die Brücke

Van Gogh's work astonished a group of young early 20th century German artists known as *Die Brücke*, meaning "the bridge." They saw in van Gogh's distorted lines, strong colors and rough brushstrokes an ideal way to express their own emotional response to what they saw and experienced.

Erich Heckel was a founding member of *Die Brücke*. In his painting of the River Elbe flowing through the German town of Dresden (right), the water ripples in a riot of colors, a bridge is picked out in red and the sky is painted with brushstrokes sweeping in every direction.

The Elbe at Dresden, Erich Heckel, 1905

The Starry Night, 1889

Creative copies

During winter at the asylum, it was far too cold to paint outdoors. Van Gogh wanted to work on studies of figures, but had no models. Instead, he spent his time painting copies of prints by his favorite artists, including Rembrandt, Delacroix and Millet.

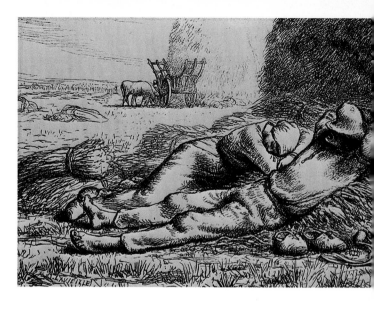

Noonday Rest, Jean-François Millet, 1866

Bursting with color

Van Gogh carefully copied the composition and details of the black-and-white prints. In his own distinctive brushstrokes, he used a combination of complementary colors to give the same sort of contrast between the light and dark areas as the original.

In *Noon: Rest from Working* (below) van Gogh copied a Millet print of farm workers dozing in the shade of a haystack (above). In van Gogh's colorful painting, the blues of the sleeping figures in the painting suggest their calm and coolness in the shade of the orange haystack. The strong blue sky contrasts with the bright yellow of the cut field behind, suggesting the fierceness of the midday summer sun.

Noon: Rest from Working (after Millet), 1890

Painter on the Road to Tarascon, 1888

Portrait of the artist

Van Gogh was not alone in copying other artists' works. The British artist Francis Bacon (1909–1992) made nine different copies of one of van Gogh's self-portraits.

Van Gogh's original shows him striding out in a straw hat along a tree-lined country road, laden with his easel, paints and a canvas, looking for a view to paint. The artist looks relaxed and determined and the colors are bright and warm.

This picture was destroyed by a firebomb in Dresden during the Second World War (1939–1945), so Bacon only ever saw a color print of it.

In all of Bacon's versions, van Gogh looks hunched, despairing and lonely. In some of the studies, Bacon included trees.

In one version (right), all details of the background have gone, leaving only a series of strongly-colored stripes to represent the sunny landscape.

 Art *What similarities and differences can you see between these two paintings?*

Study for a Portrait of van Gogh V, Francis Bacon, 1957

Bacon, like van Gogh, tried to do something new in painting, which was not immediately understood. He too wanted to paint things as he felt them to be. Perhaps Bacon felt that van Gogh represented the struggle of a lonely artist trying to find his way in an unsympathetic world.

Last months

Van Gogh despaired of ever getting better at the asylum in Saint Rémy. He decided to move north to Auvers-sur-Oise, a town near Paris, to be cared for by Dr. Gachet. Gachet had looked after other artists that van Gogh knew, including Renoir and Monet. Van Gogh also wanted to be closer to his brother Theo, who had recently had a son.

Doctor Gachet

Gachet was also a painter and art collector, and was interested in talking about art with van Gogh. He and his family became willing models for van Gogh's portraits.

Van Gogh painted Dr. Gachet looking slightly sad and deep in thought in *Portrait of Doctor Gachet* (right). The sprigs of foxgloves in the foreground are a symbol of Dr. Gachet's interest in homeopathy (a system for treating illnesses), as well as the healing powers of nature.

Portrait of Doctor Gachet, 1890

Country scenes

In two months, van Gogh painted more than a picture a day, often panoramic views on double-square canvases, such as the work *Farms near Auvers.* In this painting, surrounded by greenery and with mossy, thatched roofs, the buildings fit snugly in harmony with nature. The subtle colors reflect the cooler northern light and the loose, patterned brushwork makes the picture feel lush and full of growth.

Farms near Auvers, 1890.

Wheatfield with Crows, 1890

The end

Van Gogh's recovery did not last. He was overcome by sadness and loneliness. The restless brushstrokes and dark colors of one of his last paintings, *Wheatfield with Crows,* express his torment. He walked into these fields and shot himself. He died two days later.

Morgenthau Plan, Anselm Kiefer, 2012

Anselm Kiefer

The huge *Morgenthau Plan* (below) by Anselm Kiefer, a contemporary German artist, owes a debt to *Wheatfield with Crows*. It is named after a Second World War U.S. plan to limit Germany's ability to create weapons and wage war in the future, by destroying its industries and transforming it back to an agricultural country. Kiefer covered a huge out-of-focus photograph with encrusted, grooved paint. He embedded real stalks of wheat into the paint.

What happened next

Theo died only six months after his brother, leaving Jo, his widow, and their young child with hundreds of van Gogh's unsold canvases, drawings and van Gogh's letters to Theo. Jo spent the rest of her life promoting van Gogh's work. By the time she died in 1925, van Gogh had become recognized as an important and influential artist.

Making his art known

Jo was determined to get van Gogh's work seen and appreciated. She lent his paintings to exhibitions in Belgium, France, the Netherlands, Germany, Austria, the UK and the USA. These often hung next to works by great modern artists, such as Gauguin, Matisse and Picasso. Now and again, she sold pictures to major museums and rich, admiring art collectors. Wherever van Gogh's pictures were seen, other artists were amazed and inspired by them.

Grazing Horses IV (The Red Horses), Franz Marc, 1911

Franz Marc

Franz Marc (1880–1916) was greatly influenced by van Gogh's use of colors. His works, mainly of animals, are known for their simplicity and vibrant, unreal colors, each chosen for their emotional and spiritual meanings. For Marc, yellow represented female happiness, blue portrayed masculinity and red meant violence.

"Van Gogh is for me the most authentic, the greatest, the most poignant painter I know. To paint a bit of the most ordinary nature, putting all one's faith and longings into it – that is the supreme achievement... Now I paint... only the simplest things... Only in them are the symbolism, the pathos, and the mystery of nature to be found."
–Franz Marc

The Van Gogh Museum

Today van Gogh's paintings hang in museums all over the world. The purpose-built Van Gogh Museum in van Gogh's home country of the Netherlands is home to the large collection that Jo's son, Vincent-Willem, inherited from her. It has 270 paintings, almost 600 drawings, documents and letters written by van Gogh, which will doubtless continue to inspire artists in the future.

De Kooning

Abstract expressionists, such as Willem de Kooning (1904–1997), took van Gogh's way of painting in an entirely new direction. There is no obvious subject or focus in de Kooning's *Composition* (right). Instead, you can feel the force of the artist himself at work. The thick brushstrokes go wildly in every direction. The vivid colors twist and clash, conjuring up a feeling of energy. Perhaps that is one of van Gogh's great legacies – showing artists who came after him the expressive potential and power of color and paint.

Visitors at the Van Gogh Museum, Amsterdam, the Netherlands

Composition, Willem de Kooning, 1955

◆ Timeline

1853 March 30 Vincent van Gogh is born in Groot-Zundert in the southern Netherlands, the eldest of six children of Theodorus van Gogh, the local clergyman, and his wife.

1857 May 1 Theo, his favorite brother, is born.

1861-9 Van Gogh attends several schools.

1869 July He starts work at the art dealer Goupil and Co. in the Hague. He begins collecting prints.

1873 May Van Gogh is transferred to London office of Goupil and Co. He visits many galleries. He becomes increasingly religious.

1875 May He is transferred to Paris office of Goupil and Co.

1876 January Van Gogh leaves Goupil and Co. April–December, he works as a teacher and preacher in England.

1877 January–April Van Gogh works in a bookshop in Dordrecht.

May He studies for a theological exam at Amsterdam University, which he fails.

1878 August He takes a course to become a lay preacher, but fails to qualify.

1879 January–July He works as a lay preacher in a Belgian mining area of the Boringe. Van Gogh makes sketches of miners.

November Theo is given a permanent job at Goupil in Paris.

1880 August Theo encourages van Gogh to become an artist and starts to support him financially.

October Van Gogh enrolls enrols at the Brussels Art Academy, Belgium. Studies anatomy and perspective drawing, and studies with the painter Anton Rappard.

1881 April Van Gogh moves to the family home in Etten, where he works on his landscapes and figure drawing.

December He argues with his father. Van Gogh moves to the Hague.

1882 January He takes drawing and painting lessons from Anton Mauve, his cousin, a successful painter.

Van Gogh lives with Sien Hoornik and her daughter.

August Van Gogh's family moves to Nuenen.

1883 September He breaks his relationship with Sien. He moves to Drenthe to paint.

December Van Gogh returns to Nuenen to paint.

1884-5 He paints in Nuenen, including a series of peasant heads.

1885 March 26 His father dies.

April He paints *The Potato Eaters*.

1886 January Van Gogh briefly attends the Art Acadmey in Antwerp.

February He moves to Paris to stay with Theo.

March-April He joins the studio of Fernand Cormon. He meets Toulouse-Lautrec and Emile Bernard.

June Van Gogh moves to Montmartre in Paris with Theo.

Winter Van Gogh meets Paul Gauguin.

1887 Spring He paints views of Montmartre and the banks of the Seine River, experimenting with Impressionist brushwork

Summer He paints landscapes and flower paintings.

Autumn He paints two self-portraits. He organizes an exhibition in the Restaurant of the Chalet.

1888 February He leaves Paris for Arles.

May 1 Van Gogh rents the Yellow House as a studio.

Early June He visits Sainte Marie de la

Mer to paint boats and the village.

June-July He paints harvests and flower gardens.

August He meets Joseph Roulin. Paints *Sunflowers*.

September 17 Van Gogh moves into Yellow House

October 23 Gauguin arrives in Arles.

December 23 Van Gogh has a mental breakdown. He threatens Gauguin with a razor. He cuts off his earlobe.

December 24 Van Gogh is taken to hospital. Theo arrives.

Gauguin leaves for Paris.

1889 **January 7** Van Gogh comes home from hospital.

January 9 Theo is engaged to Jo Bonger.

February Van Gogh suffers breakdowns. He is in and out of the hospital.

April 18 Theo marries Jo Bonger.

May 8 Van Gogh is admitted to the asylum at Saint Rémy. He paints garden flowers, the view of a wheatfield from his window and copies of prints by artists who inspire him. He also paints scenes of olives, cypresses and hills.

1890 **January–February** Van Gogh shows six paintings at an exhibition of Les XX in Brussels, Belgium. *The Red Vineyard* is bought by Anna Boch.

January 31 Vincent-Willem (1890–1978), son of Theo and Jo, is born..

May 16 Van Gogh moves to Auvers near Paris.

May - July He paints landscapes, gardens, flower still-lifes and portraits of Dr Gachet and his family.

July 27 Van Gogh shoots himself in the chest in a field.

July 29 He dies with Theo beside him. He is buried the next day.

September–October Theo's

health worsens.

1891 **January** Theo dies.

March Van Gogh's works are shown at the Salon des Independents in Paris. They are favorably reviewed.

1892 An exhibition of van Gogh's work is held in the Hague.

1896 Vollard, a French art dealer has a solo show of van Gogh's work in Paris – it is not a commercial success.

1901 Five van Gogh pictures are exhibited in Berlin.

1905 Exhibition of 474 works by van Gogh at the Stedelijk Museum in Amersterdam, the Netherlands.

1906 The first van Gogh paintings are exhibited in Austria.

1907 The first book reproducing van Gogh's work appeared.

1910 Van Gogh's work is first shown in England, as part of Roger Fry's exhibition, Manet and the Post-Impressionists.

1913 Van Gogh's work is included in the Armory Show, the first large exhibition of modern art in America.

1914 The first publication of van Gogh's letters to Theo are done in Dutch and German.

1924 Jo sells *Sunflowers* to the National Gallery, London.

1925 Jo van Gogh-Bonger dies. Her son, Vincent-Willem, inherits her van Gogh collection.

1960-2 Vincent-Willem founds the Van Gogh Foundation to keep the collection intact. All works and documents are offered on permanent loan to the Dutch state.

1973 Purpose-built Van Gogh Museum opens in Amsterdam. Houses world's largest collection of his works.

1990 Van Gogh's *Portrait of Doctor Gachet* sold for a record $82.5 million.

Glossary

Abstract Expressionism an art movement that developed in New York after the Second World War. Artists tried to depict universal emotions through the physical activity of painting

asylum a place where people are treated for mental disorders

canvas a piece of coarse, stretched cloth that artists use for oil paintings

complementary colors colors that have maximum contrast between each other. The basic pairs for artists are red and green, blue and orange, and yellow and purple

composition the arrangement of shape, form and space in a painting

contrast the big difference in light and shade or colors in an artwork

easel the stand on which artists support a canvas

engraving a print created from a metal plate with a image cut into its surface, which is inked and pressed on to a sheet of paper

Fauve French for "wild beast." The nickname given to the artists, such as Henri Matisse, painting between about 1905–10 in very bright and clashing colors unrelated to the actual subjects of their pictures

hallucinations seeing or hearing things that aren't really there

illustration a picture for a book, magazine or newspaper.

impasto paint that has been thickly brushed, to create rough raised parts

Impressionism an art style (c.1874–1876) in which artists painted mostly outdoors, capturing fleeting moments and changing light using vivid colors and dappled brushstrokes

landscape a painting of the countryside.

model someone who sits still in a particular pose for an artist to draw or paint

Morgenthau Plan a plan proposed by the U.S. after the Second World War. It aimed to strip Germany of its industry and make it an agricultural country to prevent it from ever being able to wage war again

oil paint a glossy type of paint made by mixing pigments with a quick-drying oil. Oil paint can be applied thick, straight from the tube or thinned with white spirit or turpentine

palette the flat wooden board on which artists lay out and mix their oil paints. It can also mean an artist's usual choice of colors

panoramic an extensive view, such as of a landscape, looking in all directions

peasant a person who earns a small wage working in the countryside, such as a farm worker

peat decayed plant material. It can be used to grow plants or burned to use as a fuel

perspective a way that artists represent people, places and objects in a painting or drawing to make them appear solid or three-dimensional

perspective frame a viewfinder made of a wooden frame on legs with horizontal, vertical and diagonal lines, which van Gogh used as a guide for drawing in perspective

Pointillism a painting technique where the artist paints individual dots of color on the canvas. From a distance, the dots merge into a picture

portrait an image of a person, often head and shoulders, which tries to capture something of his or her personality

self-portrait a portrait that artists make of themselves

still life a picture of a group of objects, such as fruit, flowers, books, tools or crockery that an artist has often carefully arranged

symbol something, such as the image of an object, that stands for something else, such as an emotion

texture the surface quality of a painting, such as rough or smooth

watercolor a painting created with colors (called pigments) diluted with water

woodblock print a print created from a block of wood with a picture cut into it, which is inked and pressed on to a sheet of paper

Selected works

Portrait of Père Tanguy (p.19)

Van Gogh was obsessed with Japanese prints, because they appeared to show Japan as a place of beauty, simplicity, tranquility and color – a perfect utopia. He and his brother became avid collectors, amassing more than 350 woodblock prints. Their pure colors, strong outlines and unusual perspectives inspired van Gogh to work with more vivid colors placed side by side.

Behind his *Portrait of Père Tanguy* (page 19), van Gogh included his own versions of some of the prints he most admired. Behind Père Tanguy's head are two prints by the famous printmaker Utagama Hiroshige (1797–1858) – one of Mount Fuji, Japan's famous mountain, and another of a cherry tree. Behind Tanguy's left elbow is a print of a courtesan by Kesai Eisen (1790–1848), an image which van Gogh liked so much that he made his own painted copy of it.

When van Gogh moved to the south of France, he felt he had found a place like Japan. In a letter to his friend Emil Bernard, he wrote, "… this part of the world seems to me as beautiful as Japan for the clearness of the atmosphere and the gay color effects."

Self-Portait as an Artist (p.23)

Van Gogh painted 43 self-portraits altogether. The picture is the only one that shows him with all the tools of his trade, perhaps a statement of van Gogh's confidence as an artist after his two years in Paris. Wearing a blue smock to protect his clothes from paint splashes, he stands in front of an easel with a stretched canvas propped on it, holding a palette of pure colors and a variety of different-sized paintbrushes. Van Gogh obviously put his easel near a window, so that light shone on to the right-hand side of his head – notice his use of paler colors to make glints of light on his hair, neck and forehead and to add shine to his nose.

This work is a good example of van Gogh's then newly-developed distinctive style of brushwork using bold, directional, rhythmical strokes. The thick, broken, criss-cross brushstrokes suggest the coarse texture of his smock. His beard and moustache are mostly painted with long vertical marks. Curved brushstrokes define the contours on his face, hand and hair. The daubs of paint on the palette are thick and raised, just as he often applied the paint in his pictures.

Sunflowers (p.28)

The sunflower is the flower most associated with van Gogh. He even remarked that "the sunflower is mine." Of all his paintings, *Sunflowers* is the most widely reproduced. While living in Paris, van Gogh had painted four still lifes of sunflowers – cut and lying on their sides. He took up this theme again in Arles, painting a series of pictures of sunflowers in a vase, with the flowers arranged slightly differently in each one. For van Gogh, the sunflower was the emblem of the south of France and its sunshine and a tribute to Monticelli, the flower painter (see p.20), who had come from this area.

In 1889, van Gogh painted three identical copies of his sunflower pictures, intending to display them with the originals as "lampholders or candelabras" on either side of his several versions of Madame Roulin (see one version on p.27), to intensify the colors of her head.

Wheatfield with Crows (p.41)

Many of van Gogh's landscapes depict a particular place (see p.24, 25, 34 and 36) or combine the real with imaginary (see p.37), transformed into his own personal vision. However, there is nothing specific to pinpoint where van Gogh painted *Wheatfield with Crows* although we know it was painted near Auvers. The picture reveals no clues about this particular place.

Instead, with its dark, threatening sky, three empty paths leading off in totally different directions and quivering ears of wheat, this landscape could perhaps be interpreted as an expression of van Gogh's inner conflicts and his sense of feeling utterly alone. Even the crows are flying away from him into the far distance. The strong contrast in heightened color between the bright yellow field and the dark blue sky intensify the uneasy atmosphere of this work.

For More Information

Books

Essential Artists: Van Gogh by David Spence (Ticktock Books, 2010)
Eyewitness Books: Van Gogh by Bruce Bernard (DK Publishing, 1999)
Great Artists of the World: Vincent van Gogh by Alix Wood (Franklin Watts, 2015)
In the Picture with Vincent van Gogh by Iain Zaczek (Wayland, 2014)

Websites

Because of the changing nature of Internet links, Rosen Publishing has developed an online list of websites related to the subject of this book. This site is updated regularly. Please use this link to access the list:

http://www.rosenlinks.com/ART/Gogh

Index